UNITED STATES NAVAL AVIATION PATCHES

AIRCRAFT/ATTACK SQUADRONS/HELICOPTER SQUADRONS

MICHAEL L. ROBERTS

Schiffer Military/Aviation History
Atglen, PA

Acknowledgements

The following are honorably mentioned for giving me the encouragement needed for this project:

Doug Barnard	Robert Dugger	Dave Robinson
David Bernstein	Richard Hassler	Dale Stockam
Robert Biondi	John Lombardo	James Townley
William Cain	Keith Morey	Lloyd Walton
Stan Chin	J.L. Pete Morgan	Wayne Weidner

The patches depicted in this book are from the author's personal collection and are presented for historical purposes only, and to serve as a guide for historians, collectors, and designers.

This book is not intended to be the complete authority on the subject. It depicts over 1000 patches from World War II to the present.

The images on pages 6, 35, 38, 84, the front cover and endsheets are official U.S. Navy photographs.

Book Design by Michael L. Roberts & Robert Biondi.

Library of Congress Catalog Number: 95-67624

Printed in China.
ISBN: 0-88740-801-X

Published by Schiffer Publishing Ltd.
77 Lower Valley Road
Atglen, PA 19310
Please write for a free catalog.
This book may be purchased from the publisher.
Please include $2.95 postage.
Try your bookstore first.

Foreword

Insignias are the modern form of heraldry of the knights of old. In the armed services insignias serve as a form of shorthand that identifies an individual's service, rank, authority, specialty and organization. The organizational insignia, from the plain to very involved design, expresses a pride in oneself and his or her organization. From this pride springs self-discipline, the essence of respect for self, for service and for country.

The first semi-official Navy organizational insignias began to appear in the fledging Naval Aeronautical Organization in the early twenties with the establishment of the Bureau of Aeronautics in 1921 and a year later the formation of fighting, scouting, observation, seaplane patrol and torpedo plane squadrons. By 1927, the now familiar High Hat, Felix the Cat and VF-2's Flying Chiefs squadron insignias began appearing on the sides of the Navy's nimble, brightly colored biplane fighters. By the beginning of World War II all Navy aviation squadrons, most Naval and Reserve air stations, and even aircraft carriers had distinctive insignias.

During the Second World War aviation squadrons, surface ships and submarines, and shore establishment organizational insignias abound, establishing a high esprit de corps within each individual in that unit. Donald Duck, Mickey Mouse, Bugs Bunny and a host of other characters truly went to war with all branches of the armed services on the sides of tanks, planes and ships bridges. In fact in 1943, the Navy told its squadrons to knock off using Donald Duck so often for proposed insignias.

I remember all the displays of insignias in *Life* Magazine ads and collecting bottle caps and stickers from boxes of cereal during the war that had aviation insignias on them. We all knew what the insignias of the Flying Tigers, Eagle squadron, 94th Fighter and VF-31 squadrons looked like, what kind of planes they flew and how they performed in combat. When I grew up I was able turn my childhood dream into reality when I became a Naval Aviator. Acquiring that first patch in Training Squadron One and having it sewn on my flight jacket meant I had arrived and was truly a part of that unit. As my career progressed, so did the number of patches on my flight jacket until I ran out of room. Each patch on my jacket, as well as those that adorn the jackets of my fellow Naval Aviators, aircrew, and squadron/ship mates have a special memory and, in many cases, a long history behind them.

My interest in insignias is historical and I was fortunate to be able to continue to gather information on Navy and Marine Corps aviation organizations while I was in the Navy. Frequent trips to Washington, D.C., allowed me to spend considerable time at the Naval Air and Operational Histories offices where I collected as much information as I could on Navy/Marine squadrons. I have been lucky to be able to be in a position to share much of this information as insignia editor for THE HOOK magazine, the Tailhook Association's quarterly journal of carrier aviation. In this capacity I have produced the magazine's patch page, a feature for 16 years, and answered all insignia inquiries. I quickly learned that it is next to impossible to identify every insignia because there are so many, and many are unidentifiable, even with the help of the historians at the Naval Air History office where all Navy aviation insignias are supposed to be officially approved.

This book serves as a valuable guide for the insignia collector and lovers of Navy patches in providing color pictures of past and present active and Reserve Navy aviation squadrons, ships, aircraft and shore organizations. It will help the serious collectors and those getting started to identify patches in their collections. Mike's collection of Navy insignias is vast and I thank him for sharing his collection with all of us.

Doug Siegfried, CDR USN (Ret)
THE HOOK Magazine
Insignia Editor

Contents

AIRCRAFT

A-1 Skyraider Driver
A-3 Skywarrior The Whale
A-3 Skywarrior Forever
A-3 Skywarrior
A-3 Skywarrior Killer Whale
A-3 Skywarrior 30th Anniversary 1952-1982
A-4 Skyhawk The Professionals Preference
A-4 Skyhawk The Professionals Preference

A-4 Skyhawk
A-4 Skyhawk 35th Anniversary 1953-1988
A-4 Skyhawk Plane Captain
A-4 Skyhawk Tailhooker
RA-5C Vigilante
RA-5C Vigilante Unarmed & Unafraid
A-6 Intruder
A-6 Intruder

Aircraft

A-6 Intruder
A-6 Iraqi Intruder
A-6E SWIP Intruder

A-6 Electric Intruder
A-6F Intruder
A-6E Systems/Weapons/Integration Program Intruder

A-6 Flight of the Intruder
A-6 Intruder Operation Desert Storm
A-6 Desert Storm Intruder

A-6 Intruder 25th Anniversary 1963-1988
A-6 Intruder
A-6 Intruder Made in the USA

A-6 Intruder Any Time, Any Place, Any Weather
A-6 Intruder HARM Shooter
A-6 Intruder

A-6 Intruder The Mission, Attack
A-6 Intruder Any Time Baby
A-6 Intruder Hussein Hunter

A-6A Intruder
EA-6B Prowler
EA-6 Prowler

A-6 Happy Intruders
EA-6 Prowler
EA-6 Prowler

EA-6B Prowler
EA-6 Prowler
EA-6 Prowler 20 Years Still Jammin'

EA-6B Prowler DEFTAC Qualified
A-7 Corsair II
A-7 Corsair II Fleets Finest 1966-1991

EA-6B Prowler ADVCAP
A-7E Corsair II Echo Driver
A-7 Corsair II End of an Era 1963-1990

EA-6B Prowler 20th Anniversary 1990
A-7E Corsair II Harley of the Fleet
A-12 McDonnell-Douglas/General Dynamics

A-12 Medium Attack 21st Century

C-9B Skytrain II

C-2 Greyhound COD

UC-12B Ute

C-130 Hercules

C-130 Hercules Old Guard

E-2 Hawkeye

E-2 Hawkeye
E-2C Hawkeye You Can Run, But You Can't Hide
E-2 Hawkeye NATO AWACS

E-2C Hawkeye
E-2C Hawkeye Group 2
E-2 Hawkeye 300 Hawkeye Traps

E-2 Hawkeye 1000
E-2 Hawkeye Sick em Baby
E-6A

F-3H Demon
F-4 Phantom II
F-4S Stud Phlyer

F-3H Demon Driver
F-4 Phantom II Phlyer
F-4S Phantom II USN/USMC

F-3H Demon Docotor
F-4 Phantom II Phlyer
F-4S Phantom II

F-4 Phantom II Driver

F-4 Phantom II Plane Captain

F-4 Phantom II Pherret

F-4 Phantom II Phixer

F-4 Phantom II 30th Anniversary 1958-1988

F-4 Phantom II 30th Anniversary 1958-1988

F-4 Phantom II 30th Anniversary Phabulous Phantoms 1958-1988

F-4 Phantom II 30th Anniversary 1958-1988 USN/USMC/USAF

F-4 Phantom II Phantom Phanatics

F-4 Phantom II
F-4 Phantom II 1000 Hours
F-4 Phantom II 4000 Hours

F-4 Phantom II
F-4 Phantom II 2000 Hours
F-4 Phantom II RECCE 2500 Hours

F-4S Phantom II
F-4 Phantom II 3000 Hours
F-4 Phantom II RECCE 3000 Hours

F-4 Phantom II
F-4 Phantom II 3500 Hours
F-4 Phantom II Life Support

F-4 Phantom II Avionics

F-4 Phantom II 100 Combat Missions Viet Nam

F4U Corsair

F-5 Tiger II

F-7U Cutlass

F-8 Crusader

F-8 Crusader Forever

F-8 Crusader When You're Out of F-8s, You're Out of Fighters

F-8 Crusader MiG Master

F-14 Tomcat
F-14 Tomcat Subdued
F-14 Tomcat Anytime, Baby...!

F-14 Tomcat
F-14 Tomcat Anytime, Baby...!
F-14A Plus Tomcat

F-14 Tomcat
F-14 Tomcat Anytime, Baby...!
F-14 Tomcat 1000 hours

F-14 Tomcat 2000 Hours
F-14D Tomcat A New Breed
F-14D Super Tomcat

F-14 Tomcat 2500 hours
F-14D Super Tomcat
F-14D Super Tomcat

F-14A Plus Tomcat
F-14D Tomcat Go Ahead Make My Day
F-14 Tomcat Pilot, Baby!

F-14 Tomcat R.I.O., Baby!

F-14 Tomcat Plane Captain

F-14 Tomcat Plane Captain

F-14 Tomcat 20th Anniversary 1970-1990

F-14 Tomcat Peeping Tom TARPS

F-14 Tomcat Screw with the Tomcats, You Get the Claw!

F-14 Tomcat 100 Dark Ones, Baby! Night Centurion

F-14 Tomcat 100 Times, Baby! 100 Centurion

F-14 Tomcat 600 Times, Baby! 600 Centurian
F-14 Tomcat
F-14 Tomcat Operation Desert Storm, Thief of Baghdad

F-14 Tomcat Oopack, Baby!
F-14 Tomcat Hussein Hunter
F-14 Tomcat

F-14 Tomcat Oopack, Baby!
F-14 Tomcat Operation Desert Shield
F-14 Tomcat TVSU

F-14 Tomcat
F-14 Tomcat

F-14 Tomcat
F-14 Tomcat

F-14 Tomcat
F-14 Tomcat Respice Futurum

F-14 Tomcat Cats Night Out
F-14 Tomcat
F-14 Tomcat

F-14 Tomcat TARPS Everytime, Baby...!
F-14 Tomcat
F-14 Tomcat
F-14 Tqmcat

F-14 Tomcat
F-14 Tomcat
F-14 Tomcat

F-14 Tomcat Tweakers
F-14 Tomcat Party Time Baby!
F-14 Tomcat Forever, Baby!

F-14 Tomcat Operation Desert Storm 1991 Saddam...Send More MiGs
F-14 Tomcat Flight Test
F-14 Tomcat Anytime Saddam!

F-14 Tomcat 20th Anniversary 1971-1991
F-14 Tomcat He Is My Prefered Toy
F-14 Tomcat Anytime Khadaffi!

F-14 Tomcat Operation Desert Storm
We Own the Skies

F-14 Tomcat Pray, Baby!
Operation Desert Storm

F-14 Tomcat Operation Desert Storm
You Can Run, But You'll Only Die Tired

F-14 Tomcat 20th Anniversary
Getting Better With Age

F-14 Tomcat I Smoke Camels Baby!
Operation Desert Storm

F-14 Tomcat Tomcat Tweakers

F-14 Tomcat
Go Ahead...Make My Day!

F-14 Tomcat I Smoke Camels Baby!
Operation Desert Storm

F-14 Tomcat A Tale From Two Tails...

F-16N Falcon
F-16N Falcon Navy Adversary
F/A-18 Hornet

F/A-18 Hornet Is It Cool In Here Or Is It Me
F/A-18 Hornet
F/A-18 Hornet Strike Fighter
F/A-18 Hornet Strike Fighter

F/A-18 Hornet Strike Fighter
F/A-18 Hornet
F/A-18 Hornet

F/A-18 Hornet Strike Fighter
F/A-18 Hornet Strike Fighter USN/USMC
F/A-18 Hornet 2000 Hours

F/A-18 Hornet Strike Fighter
F/A-18C/D Hornet Night Attack
F/A-18 Hornet Hornet Handler

F/A-18 Hornet
F/A-18 Hornet 1000 Hours
F/A-18 Hornet Hornet Handler, Subdued

F/A-18 Hornet Someone Under Thirty You Can Trust
F/A-18 Hornet Iraqi Stinger Desert Storm
F/A-18 Hornet Now Baby...
F/A-18 Hornet Now Baby...
F/A-18 Hornet Now Baby...
F/A-18 Hornet FLIR
F/A-18 Hornet Ferrari Driver No FO's
F/A-18 Hornet Made In The Good Old USA
F/A-18 Hornet
F/A-18 Hornet Fun Meter

F/A-18 Hornet Hussein Hunter
F-21A Kfir
SH-3H Search/Detect/Destroy

F/A-18 Hornet
SH-2F LAMPS Mark I
Sea King SH-3H

F-21A Kfir
SH-3 Sea King
H-46 Sea Knight

H-46 Sea Knight FRS Instructor
SH-60F Seahawk
SH-60 LAMPS

MH-53E Sea Dragon
SH-60F Seahawk
SH-60 LAMPS Mark III Anytime, Baby...

H-53 100 Hours FAM
SH-60 LAMPS
P-3 Orion

P-3A Orion
EP-3E Aries
P-3C Orion Update III
P-3C Orion
P-3C Orion NFO Instructor
P-3 Orion FRS Instructor Pilot
P-3 Orion FRS Instructor NFO
P-3 Orion FRS Instructor Aircrewman

S-3 Viking S-3A Viking S-3A Viking
S-3A Viking S-3 Viking S-3A Viking War Hoover T-2 Buckeye
T-2 Buckeye Air Superiority T-28 Trojan Driver T-34C Radial Interceptor

T-34 Instructor 500 Combat Free Missions
T-45 Goshawk
Desert Storm Total Resolve

T-39 Sabre Liner
T-45 Goshawk First Flight, 1990
Libya: Pay Back Is A Bitch

T-45A Goshawk
Navy MiG Killers
Fleet Air Refueling Tanker Aircraft: We Pass Gas

Missiles

Aegis
Harpoon
Harpoon
Encapsulated Harpoon
Harpoon 10th Anniversary 1977-1987
AGM-65F Maverick
Polaris
Poseidon

Poseiden

Stinger

Sparrow

Subroc

Trident

ASW Standoff

Trident

Missiles

HELICOPTER SQUADRONS

HAL-3
HAL-4
HAL-5

HAL-3 Vung Tau
HAL-4 Subdued
HAL-5

HAL-4
HAL-5
HAL-5 Subdued

HC-1 HC-1

HC-1 Detachment Point Mugu, California 1989

HC-1 Det 2 HC-1 Det 2 Operation Desert Storm 1991

HC-1 Det 3 HC-1 Det 3 HC-1 Det 4 WESTPAC 1977

HC-1 Det 6
HC-2
HC-2 Det 1 Naples, Italy

HC-1 Det 8 1969-1970
HC-2
HC-2 Det 2

HC-2
HC-2 Det 1
HC-2 Det 2

HC-2 Det 60 Mediterranean 1969

HC-2 Det 62 WESTPAC 1965

HC-2 Det 62 NATO Cruise 1969

HC-2 Det 66 WESTPAC 1972

HC-2 Det 67 Mediterranean Cruise 1970-1971

HC-2 Mediterranean Cruise 1969

HC-3

HC-3

HC-3 Plane Captain

HC-3 Det 111 WESTPAC 1976-1977

HC-3 Det 111 1976-1977

HC-4

HC-4

HC-4 Det 83 1970-1971

HC-5 — HC-5 Subdued — HC-5 Det 2

HC-5 Det 2 — HC-5 Det 5 — HC-6

HC-6 Det 1 Mediterranean 1986 — HC-6 Det 1 Mediterranean 1990-1991

HC-6 Det 2 Mediterranean/Red Sea 1991-1992
HC-6 Det 5 Mediterranean Cruise 1993
HC-7

HC-6 Det 3 Costa del Sol 1987-1988
HC-6 Det 6 1987
HC-7 Det Cubi, Philippines 1973

HC-6 Det 3 1989
HC-6 Det 8 1993-1994
HC-8

HC-8
HC-8 Team 3
HC-9

HC-8
HC-8 Team 3 1989
HC-9

HC-8 Team 2
HC-8 Det 5 Mediterranean 1986
HC-9

HC-9 | HC-11 | HC-11 Det 5 WESTPAC 1989

HC-11 Det 7 1990-1991 | HC-11 Det 8 PACEX/RIMPAC/NORPAC/WESTPAC 1989-1991 | HC-11 Det Operation Desert Storm 1990-1991

HC-11 Det 8 WESTPAC 1990-1991 | HC-11 Det 8 Operation Desert Storm 1991 | HC-16

HC-16
HCS-5
HM-12

HCS-4
HCS-5 Subdued
HM-12

HCS-4 Subdued
HCT-16
HM-12 Vertical Onboard Delivery Detachment

HM-14 HM-14
HM-14 Persian Gulf 1987-1988 HM-14 WESTPAC 1983
HM-15 Plank Owner HM-15 HM-15 Airborne Mine Counter Measures

HM-15 AMCM — HM-15 PACEX 1989

HM-16 — HM-16 Denmark 1985 — HM-18

HM-18 — HM-18 — HM-19

HS-1 HS-1 40th Anniversary 1951-1991 HS-1 Det 1
HS-1 Det 3 HS-2
HS-2

HS-2 Det A 1987 | HS-3

HS-4 | HS-4 | HS-4

HS-4 | HS-5

Helicopter Squadrons

HS-5 — HS-5 Mediterranean 1984-1985

HS-6 — HS-6 — HS-6

HS-6 — HS-6 Subdued — HS-6 Subdued

HS-6 Tiger Cruise 1984
HS-7 Round the World (attributed to)
HS-7 Night Dipping Centurion (Attributed to)

HS-6
HS-7 (Attributed to)
HS-8

HS-7
HS-7 Operation Desert Storm 1990-1991
HS-8

HS-8 Excellence in Maintenance Award

HS-8 Maintenance WESTPAC 1977-1978

HS-8 Det 4 1967

HS-8

HS-8

HS-9

HS-9 NATO 1966

HS-9 Det 66 Mediterranean 1967

HS-9 Mediterranean 1987 — HS-9 Mediterranean 1989

HS-10 — HS-10 — HS-10

HS-10 Excellence in Maintenance Award — HS-11

HS-11 | HS-11 (Attributed to) | HS-11 Det 5 1976

HS-12 | HS-12 | HS-12 Strike Rescue

HS-13 | HS-14 | HS-14

HS-14   HS-14 Operation Desert Storm   HS-14 Operation Desert Storm

HS-14 Operation Southern Watch 1992   HS-15

HS-15   HS-17

HS-17 Mediterranean 1985-1986

HS-74

HS-75

HS-75

HS-80L2

HS-84

HS-85 HS-85 HS-246
HS-742 HS-84/HS-85 Det 845 1984-1985 HSL-30
HSL-30 Det Alpha 15 HSL-31

HSL-31 Det A
HSL-32
HSL-32 Det 3 Standard Naval Force Atlantic 1984

HSL-31 Det Bravo
HSL-32 Det 1 Mediterranean 1990
HSL-32 Det 3 Mediterranean 1990

HSL-31 Det Bravo Panama 1977-1978
HSL-32 Det 2 Mediterranean 1990
HSL-32 Det 5 Counter Drug Operations 1992

HSL-32 Det 5 Mediterranean 1993 | HSL-32 Det 6 Mediterranean 1981-1982 | HSL-32 Det 6

HSL-32 Det 8 Maintenance Crew | HSL-32 Det 8 | HSL-32 Det 8 Mediterranean/Red Sea 1991

HSL-33 | HSL-33 Det 5 | HSL-33 Det 5 Drug Bustin' 1991-1992

HSL-33 Det 7
HSL-33 Det 7, Persian Gulf 1990
HSL-34

HSL-33 Det 10
HSL-34
HSL-34 Mediterranean 1985

HSL-34 Safety "S" Battle "E" 1992
HSL-34 Det 1
HSL-34 Det 5

HSL-34 Plane Captain
HSL-34 Det 1
HSL-34 Det 8 1983-1984

HSL-34 Det 1
HSL-34 Det 2 UNITAS XXVII 1986
HSL-34 Det 8

HSL-34 Det Whiskey
HSL-35 Det 5 WESTPAC 1977-1978
HSL-36

HSL-35
HSL-35 Det 6
HSL-36 Det 2

HSL-35 Det 1
HSL-35 Det 7 Operation Desert Storm 1990
HSL-36 Det 3 Mediterranean 1987

HSL-36 Det 4 Middle East Force 1989 — HSL-36 — HSL-36 Det 6 SNFL 1990

HSL-36 Det 7 Mediterranean 1990 — HSL-36 Det 8 Mediterranean 1987 — HSL-36 Det 8

HSL-36 Det 9 Mediterranean 1988 — HSL-36 Det 9 Mediterranean 1990

HSL-37 — HSL-37 — HSL-37 Det 1 WESTPAC 1984
HSL-37 Det 3 — HSL-37 Det 10 WESTPAC 1982/1983 — HSL-40
HSL-41 — HSL-41 — HSL-42

HSL-42 Det 1 Mediterranean 1985

HSL-42 Mediterranean 1987

HSL-42 Det 1 SNFL 1987

HSL-42 Det 2 MEF 1988

HSL-42 Det 2 World Tour 1991-1992

HSL-42 Det 3 Mediterranean 1989

HSL-42 Det 3 Mediterranean/Red Sea 1991

HSL-42 Det 3 Mediterranean 1993

HSL-42 Det 4 Mediterranean 1985 | HSL-42 Det 4 MEF 1989 | HSL-42 Det 5 Blue Nose 1985

HSL-42 Det 5 North Star/Mediterranean 1991-1992 | HSL-42 Det 6 Mediterranean 1989 | HSL-42 Det 7 Mediterranean 1993

HSL-42 Det 7 | HSL-42 Det 8 Mediterranean 1986 | HSL-42 Det 8 MEF 1991

HSL-42 Det 8 Mediterranean 1993
HSL-42 Det 9 SNFL 1987
HSL-42 Det 9
HSL-42 Det 9 MEF 1990
HSL-42 Det 10 MEF 1990
HSL-42 Det 10 Mediterranean 1992
HSL-43
HSL-43 Det 2

HSL-43 Det 2

HSL-43 Det 2B

HSL-43 Det 3 WESTPAC 1988-1989

HSL-43 Det 7 WESTPAC 1990

HSL-43 Det 10 1990

HSL-44

HSL-44 "E" 1989

HSL-44 Operation Desert Storm

HSL-44 Det 1
HSL-44 Det 2
HSL-44 Det 3 1993

HSL-44 Det 1 MEF 1993
HSL-44 Det 3 MEF 1987
HSL-44 Det 4 Persian Gulf 1990

HSL-44 Det 2 Mediterranean 1991
HSL-44 Det 3 Middle East 1991-1992
HSL-44 Det 4 MEF 1992

HSL-44 Det 5 MEF 1992
HSL-44 Det 7
HSL-44 Det 8 Red Sea/Mediterranean 1993

HSL-44 Det 5 MEF 1992 Subdued
HSL-44 Det 7 Mediterranean 1992
HSL-44 Det 9 Mediterranean 1992

HSL-44 Det 6 Mediterranean 1993
HSL-44 Det 8 Operation Desert Storm 1990
HSL-44 Det 9 Mediterranean 1992

HSL-44 Det 10 Persian Gulf 1992
HSL-45 Det 1
HSL-45 Det 3 1987-1988

HSL-45
HSL-45 Det 1 1992-1993
HSL-45 Det 3

HSL-45 WESTPAC 1990
HSL-45 Det 2
HSL-45 Det 4 MEF 1987-1988

HSL-45 Det 4 WESTPAC 1992-1993
HSL-45 Det 6
HSL-45 Det 10

HSL-45 Det 5 WESTPAC 1991
HSL-45 Det 7 WESTPAC 1992
HSL-45 (attributed to)

HSL-45 Det 5 Subdued
HSL-45 Det 7
HSL-45 Det 12 1989-1990

HSL-45 Det 13 — HSL-46 — HSL-46 Det 1 Mediterranean 1989

HSL-46 "E" 1990-1991 — HSL-46 Det 2 MEF 1989

HSL-46 Det 3 MEF 1989 — HSL-46 Det 2 MEF 1993 — HSL-46 Det 3 Mediterranean 1992

HSL-46 Det 4 Mediterranean 1990
HSL-46 Det 6 1991-1992
HSL-46 Det 9 Mediterranean 1992

HSL-46 Det 5 Joint Task Group 1993
HSL-46 Det 7
HSL-47

HSL-46 Det 6
HSL-46 Det 8
HSL-47

HSL-47 Det 1 Bravo

HSL-47 Det 3 Ford Aerospace

HSL-47 Det 3 1992

HSL-47 Det 5

HSL-47 Det 6 WESTPAC/Persian Gulf 1991

HSL-47 Det 18

HSL-47 Det 9 WESTPAC 1990

HSL-48

HSL-48 Plane Captain
HSL-48 Det 2 Mediterranean 1993
HSL-48 Det 5 Mediterranean/Red Sea 1993

HSL-48 Det 1 Mediterranean 1990
HSL-48 Det 2 Operation Desert Shield
HSL-48 Det 6 MEF 1992

HSL-48 Det 1 MEF 1993
HSL-48 Det 3
HSL-48 Det 9 UNITAS XXXIV

HSL-49
HSL-49 Det 5 WESTPAC/Persian Gulf 1993-1994
HSL-84

HSL-49 Det 1
HSL-51
HSL-94

HSL-49 Det 1
HSL-74
HSL-94 Det 2

HT-8

HT-8

HT-8

HT-18

HU-1 Det Mike WESTPAC 1965-1966

HU-2

HU-2 Det 62 Mediterranean 1963-1964

HU-4

Fixed Wing Squadrons

ATU-301 FASRON-104 VA-2

VA2-F1 VA-8

VA-12 VA-12 VA-12

VA-15	VA-15 Far East 1985-1986	VA-15 (attributed to)
VA-22	VA-22	VA-23

VA-23 Far East 1968
VA-27 Safety "S" Battle "E" 1986
VA-34

VA-25
VA-34
VA-34 Night Vision Goggles

VA-27
VA-34
VA-35

VA-35 Operation Desert Storm 1991 (attributed to)
VA-36
VA-37

VA-36
VA-37
VA-37 Battle "E" 1989

VA-36
VA-37
VA-42

VA-42 TC-4C — VA-42 Visual Weapons Detachment El Centro, California/Yuma, Arizona — VA-44

VA-45 — VA-46 — VA-46 Battle "E" 1990

VA-46 Operation Desert Storm (Attributed to) — VA-52 — VA-52

VA-52 VA-52 VA-52
VA-52 VA-55 VA-55
VA-55 VA-55

VA-55 | VA-55 Mediterranean 1985-1986 | VA-55 "E" 1985-1986

VA-55 Tanker Centurion (Attributed to) | VA-56 | VA-56

VA-56 Top Gun 1959 | VA-64

VA-65 Mediterranean 1970-1971

VA-65

VA-65

VA-65 Battle "E" 1991

VA-65 Operation Desert Storm 1991

VA-65 North Atlantic/Mediterranean 1975-1976

VA-66

VA-72

VA-75

VA-75 Mediterranean 1974-1975

VA-75 Mediterranean 1977

VA-75 Gonzo Station 1982

VA-75 Operation Desert Storm 1991

VA-75

VA-75 50th Anniversary 1943-1993 | VA-76 | VA-81

VA-81 | VA-81 Last Corsair Cruise 1987

VA-82 | VA-82 McClusky Award 1976 | VA-83

VA-85
VA-85 Operation Desert Storm 1991 (Attributed to)
VA-87

VA-85 Retention/Energy 1979-1980
VA-86
VA-93

VA-85 Mediterranean/Arctic Cruise 1981
VA-87
VA-94

VA-95 | VA-95 Operation Desert Storm | VA-95

VA-95 Battle "E" and Safety "S" 1990 | VA-95 Operation Southern Watch 1993 (attributed to)

VA-97 | VA-97 | VA-97 Safety "S" 1976

VA-97 Safety "S" 1983 VA-104 VA-105
VA-105 Battle "E" 1984 VA-106
VA-113 VA-115

VA-115 NORPAC 1983 — VA-115 40th Anniversary 1948-1988 — VA-115 Olympics 1988
VA-115 Persian Gulf 1991 — VA-115 — VA-115 Operation Desert Storm
VA-115 Permanent WESTPACers — VA-115 50th Anniversary 1942-1992

VA-116 VA-122 VA-122 Det Fallon

VA-125 VA-127

VA-126

VA-127 VA-127 Pacific Fleet Adversary

VA-128 | VA-128 | VA-133

VA-144 | VA-145

VA-145 | VA-145 WESTPAC 1976 | VA-145 Derby Champions 1985-1988

VA-145 Operation Desert Storm 1991 VA-145 Last Ride Around the Horn 1952-1993 VA-146
VA-146 WESTPAC 1988-1989 VA-147
VA-152 VA-152

VA-153 VA-153 VA-153

VA-153 Blue Tail Fly VA-155 VA-155

VA-155 VA-155 Battle "E" and McClusky 1992

VA-163
VA-165

VA-164
VA-172

VA-165
VA-165 (attributed to)

VA-174
VA-174 Det El Centro, California
VA-176 Battle "E" 1988-1990

VA-175
VA-185

VA-174 End of an Era A-7 Corsair 1966-1988
VA-176
VA-185

VA-192

VA-195

VA-196

VA-192 Iwakuni, Japan 1985

VA-196

VA-195

VA-196

VA-196

VA-196 World Cruise 1983
VA-203
VA-205 Attack Transition 1990-1991

VA-196 WESTPAC 1988-1989
VA-204
VA-209

VA-196 WESTPAC 1988-1989
VA-205
VA-212

VA-215 VA-303 VA-216

VA-304 VA-304 VA-304

VA-304 VA-304

Fixed Wing Squadrons

VA-305 VA-305

VA-811

VA-892 VA-912

VA-0686

Fixed Wing Squadrons

VA-0689	VA-1287	VA-2082
VA-2267	VA-46/VA-72 American Legend 1965-1991	VA-115/VA-185 Loading Det 1988

VA(AW)-33 VA(AW)-33

VAH-1 VAH-1 VAH-2

VAH-2 VAH-2

VAH-3 VAH-3 VAH-4

VAH-4 Airpac Bomb Derby Champions 1959 VAH-4 Det Bravo

VAH-4 Det Golf 1967 VAH-4 Det November

VAH-5 VAH-5 VAH-6
VAH-6 Det 33 7th Fleet 1957-1958 VAH-7
VAH-7 VAH-8 VAH-9

VAH-9 VAH-10 VAH-11
VAH-13 VAH-15
VAH-16 VAH-16 Det Alfa

VAH-21 Project Trim
RVAH-3
RVAH-5

VAH-123
RVAH-3
RVAH-6

RVAH-1
RVAH-5
RVAH-6 WESTPAC 1966

RVAH-7
RVAH-11
RVAH-13

RVAH-9
RVAH-12
RVAH-13

RVAH-13 10th Anniversary 1961-1971
RVAH-12
RVAH-13 WESTPAC 1972-1973

RVAH-14 VAHM-10 VAK-208

VAK-308 VAK-308 Around the World in 1984

VAL-4 VAL-4

VAN-12 (attributed to) VAN-12 VAP-61
VAP-62 VAQ-33 VAQ-33 (attributed to)
VAQ-34 VAQ-34

VAQ-35 VAQ-129 VAQ-130
VAQ-130 VAQ-130 Operation Desert Storm 1991 VAQ-130 Operation Desert Storm 1991 (attributed to)
VAQ-130 Dalmation/Station 1992-1993 VAQ-131 VAQ-131

VAQ-131 Indian Ocean
VAQ-132 Battle "E" 1992
VAQ-134

VAQ-132
VAQ-133
VAQ-134 WESTPAC/Indian Ocean 1984-1985

VAQ-132 Operation Desert Storm (Attributed to)
VAQ-133 Mediterranean/Suez/Indian Ocean 1981
VAQ-134 WESTPAC 1992-1993

VAQ-135
VAQ-136 Mediterranean 1978-1979
VAQ-136

VAQ-135 Operation Southern Watch 1993
VAQ-136 Operation Desert Storm 1991
VAQ-137

VAQ-136
VAQ-136
VAQ-137 Plane Captain 200 Launches

VAQ-138
VAQ-139
VAQ-140

VAQ-138
VAQ-139 EA-6B
VAQ-141

VAQ-138 Mediterranean/Caribbean 1985
VAQ-139 Operation Desert Storm (attributed to)
VAQ-142

VAQ-208

VAQ-308

VAQ-209

VAQ-309

VAQ-209

VAQ-309

Barrier Pacific

Barrier Pacific Det Midway Island

VAW-11

VAW-11

VAW-11 Det Echo 1964

VAW-11 Det Echo 1964

VAW-12

VAW-11 Det Echo Plane Captains 1964

VAW-12 Det 33 Mediterranean 1959

VAW-13

VAW-12 Det 60

VAW-13 VAW-78 VAW-78
VAW-88 VAW-88 Caribbean 1982 VAW-110
VAW-111 VAW-111

VAW-111 Det 31
VAW-112
VAW-113

VAW-112
VAW-112 Subdued
VAW-113

VAW-112
VAW-112 World Cruise 1987
VAW-113

VAW-113 | VAW-113 Group II | VAW-113
VAW-113 | VAW-113 | VAW-114
VAW-114 | VAW-115 | VAW-116

VAW-116
VAW-117
VAW-117 (attributed to)

VAW-116
VAW-117
VAW-117 Battle "E" 1982-1983

VAW-116 Mediterranean 1978
VAW-117
VAW-117 WESTPAC 1982-1983 (attributed to)

VAW-120
VAW-121
VAW-122

VAW-120
VAW-121 (attrit uted to)
VAW-122

VAW-120
VAW-121 Battle "E" 1979-1981
VAW-122

VAW-122 VAW-122 Mediterranean Sunset Tour 1991 VAW-123
VAW-123 Mediterranean 1976 VAW-123 Mediterranean/Indian Ocean 1993-1994
VAW-124 VAW-124 VAW-125

VAW-125 (attributed to)
VAW-126
VAW-126 "Sometimes Baby..." (attributed to)
VAW-126 Mediterranean 1986-1987
VAW-127
VAW-307
VAW-0285
VAW-1086

RVAW-110 RVAW-120 VB-4
VB-11 VB-20
VB-84 VB-135

VC-1
VC-1 Adversary
VC-3 Det San Clemente Islands

VC-1
VC-2
VC-3 Chukar Pups 1981

VC-1 Adversary
VC-3
VC-5

VC-5	VC-5	VC-5 Adversary
VC-5	VC-5 Drone Division	VC-6
VC-6	VC-7	VC-8

VC-8
VC-10
VC-10

VC-8
VC-10
VC-10

VC-8 Adversary
VC-10
VC-12

VC-12 VC-12 VC-12

VC-13 VC-21

VC-33 VC-33 (attributed to)

VC-33 Det 38 World Cruise 1953-1954

VC-35 VAN Det Korea 1952

VC-61

VC-70

VC-885

VCS-2

VCS-8

VCS-6

Fixed Wing Squadrons

Duck on Bomb

3rd Squadron-Air Wing 3

Helo-Penguin

Det 5 NATO Cruise 1985

Mr. Ed's Mediterranean Cruise 1993

Index

Fixed Wing Squadrons

GLOSSARY

AC	Aircrew
ACLS	Automated Carrier Landing System
ACM	Aircraft Maneuvers (Dogfight)
AMCM	Airborne Mine Counter Measures
Around the Horn	Cape Horn, South America
ASW	Anti-Submarine Warfare
ASWOC	Anti-Submarine Warfare Operations Center
BaltOps	Baltic Sea Operations
BIOT	British Indian Ocean Territory
Blue Nose	North Atlantic
Centurian	The one hundred mark associated with carrier landings
COD	Carrier Onboard Delivery (Greyhound A/C)
Comfair	Commander Fleet Air
CTF	Commander Task Force
CVBG	Carrier Battle Group
CVSM	Ship Maintenance Program
DASH	Drone Anti-Submarine Warfare Helicopter
Det	Detachment
"E"	Battle Readiness Award
FCLP	Field Carrier Landing Practice
FRS	Fleet Replacement Squadron
HornEx	Cape Horn Exercise
Icex	North/South Pole Exercise
IO	Indian Ocean
JTG	Joint Task Group
LAMPS	Light Airborne Multi-Purpose System
Last Ride	Scheduled for decomissioning
Med	Mediterranean Sea
MEF	Middle East Force
MIF	Maritime Interdiction Force
NFO	Naval Flight Officer
Nocturian	Night Centurion
NorPac	Northern Pacific
NVG	Night Vision Goggles
Pacex	Pacific Exercise
PC	Plane Captain
Plankowner	An individual that was onboard the unit at commisioning
Polywog	Crossing the international dateline
RimPac	Pacific Rim
RIO	Radar Intercept Officer
"S"	Safety Award
S & R	Search and Rescue
Shellback	Crossing the equator
SLEP	Service Life Extension Program
SNFL	Standard Naval Force Atlantic
Sunset Cruise	Scheduled for decommisioning
TARPS	Tactical Air Reconnaissance Pod System
The Ditch	Suez Canal
Tiger Cruise	Navy league goes aboard ship in Hawaii and rides back to U.S.
TVSU	Television Surveillance Unit
UNITAS	Annual joint exercise with South America
VertiRep	Vertical Replenishment (Helicopter)
VOD	Vertical Onboard Delivery (Helicopter)
WestPac	Western Pacific

Also from the publisher

FLIGHT HANDBOOK

Navy Models

F9F-6, -6P AIRCRAFT

This facsimile reprint is the actual flight manual for the F9F-6 Cougar U.S. Navy fighter aircraft. Operational aspects covered are: flight characterstics, emergency procedures, all-weather operations, communications procedures, reconnnaissance systems, flight crew coordination, evaluation, and performance data.

Size: 8 1/2" x 11" photographs, drawings, diagrams, charts, graphs
192 pages, soft cover
ISBN: 0-88740-778-1 $19.95

PILOT'S HANDBOOK

Navy Models

F4U-5, -5N, -5NL, 5P AIRCRAFT

This facsimile reprint is the actual pilot's handbook for the F4U-5, -5N, -5NL and -5P Corsair U.S. Navy fighter aircraft. Operational aspects covered are: flight characterstics, emergency procedures, all-weather operations, communications procedures, weapons systems, evaluation, and performance data.

Size: 8 1/2" x 11" photographs, drawings, diagrams, charts, graphs
112 pages, soft cover
ISBN: 0-88740-821-4 $19.95